DRA... ...S
DRA... ...NS
AND OT... ...TURES

Steve Beaumont

W
FRANKLIN WATTS

Published in 2011 by Franklin Watts

Copyright © 2011 Arcturus Publishing Limited

Franklin Watts
338 Euston Road
London NW1 3BH

Franklin Watts Australia
Level 17/207 Kent Street
Sydney, NSW 2000

Artwork and text: Steve Beaumont and Dynamo Limited
Editors: Kate Overy and Joe Harris
Designer: Steve Flight

A CIP catalogue record for this book is available from the British Library

Dewey Decimal Classification Number: 743.8'7

ISBN: 978 1 4451 0451 5
SL001626EN

Printed in China

Franklin Watts is a division of Hachette Children's Books,
an Hachette Livre UK company.
www.hachettelivre.co.uk

CONTENTS

GETTING STARTED

Before you can start creating fantastic artwork, you need some basic equipment. Take a look at this guide to help you get started.

PAPER

Layout Paper

It's a good idea to buy inexpensive plain A4 or A3 paper from a stationery shop for all of your practice work. Most professional illustrators use cheaper paper for basic layouts and practice sketches, before producing their final artworks on more costly material.

Cartridge Paper

This is heavy-duty, high-quality drawing paper, ideal for your final drawings. You don't have to buy the most expensive brand – most art or craft shops will stock their own brand or a student range. Unless you're thinking of turning professional, this will do just fine.

Watercolour Paper

This paper is made from 100 per cent cotton, so it is much higher quality than wood-based paper. Most art shops stock a large range of weights and sizes. Either 250 grams per square metre (gsm) or 300 gsm will be fine.

PENCILS

Buy a variety of graphite (lead) pencils ranging from soft (6B) to hard (2H). Hard pencils last longer and leave less lead on the paper. Soft pencils leave more lead and wear down quickly. HB pencils are a good medium option to start with. Spend time drawing with each pencil and get used to its qualities.

Another product to try is the mechanical pencil, where you click the lead down the barrel using the button at the top. Try 0.5 mm lead thickness to start with. These pencils are good for fine detail work.

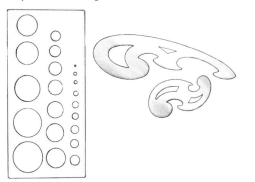

CIRCLE TEMPLATE

This is useful for drawing small circles.

FRENCH CURVES

These are available in several shapes and sizes, and are useful for drawing curves.

INKING AND COLOURING

Once you have finished your pencil drawing, you need to add ink and colour. Here are some tools you can use to achieve different results.

PENS
There are plenty of high-quality pens on the market these days that will do a decent job of inking. It's important to experiment with a range of different ones to decide which you find the most comfortable to work with.

You may find you end up using a combination of pens to produce your finished artworks. Remember to use a pen with watertight ink if you want to colour your illustrations with a watercolour or ink wash. It's usually a good idea to use watertight ink anyway as there's nothing worse than having your nicely inked drawing ruined by an accidental drop of water!

PANTONE MARKERS
These are versatile, double-ended pens that give solid, bright colours. You can use them as normal marker pens or with a brush and a little water like a watercolour pen.

BRUSHES
Some artists like to use a fine brush for inking linework. This takes a bit more practice and patience to master, but the results can be very satisfying. If you want to try your hand at brushwork, you should invest in some high-quality sable brushes.

WATERCOLOURS AND GOUACHE
Most art stores stock a wide range of these products from professional to student quality.

MASTERCLASS: SCALES AND SNAKES

DRAWING SCALES

It's difficult to draw scales on a curved body. Here is a way that will make it easy for you to complete a detailed drawing. It's called the brick method.

❶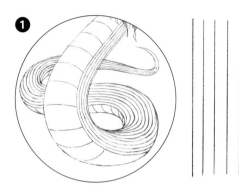

Start by drawing a series of parallel lines.

❷

Next add short, staggered lines joining together the parallel lines, as if you were drawing a brick wall.

❸

Round off the brick shapes to create the scales. Keep on doing this until you have a complete snake's skin.

❹

The final result is incredibly realistic. Take a look at the basilisk on pages 14–19 for the full impressive effect.

SNAKE HEADS

When you come to draw the Medusa on pages 20–25, you will see that the snakes on her head are quite small. Here is a larger snake for you to study and copy.

❶ **❷** **❸**

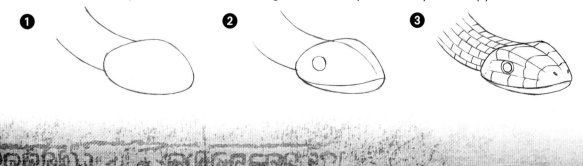

MASTERCLASS: WING STRUCTURE

DRAGON WINGS

A dragon's wings are similar to those of a bat. So it makes sense to base the construction of a dragon's wings on this small night-flying animal.

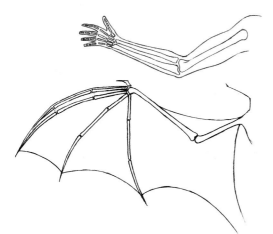

The structure of a bat's wing is similar to that of a human arm and hand. The bones of the wing form the shape of an arm and bend in the same places. The end of the wing is like a human hand with four fingers and a short thumb. The difference is that a bat has a thin membrane stretching over this structure.
On this basis, you can break down drawing a bat's wing into the simple steps below.

Picture 1 First plot out the wing. You need a short 'thumb' at the top and four longer 'fingers'.

Picture 2 Turn these into proper shapes by adding a second line close to the first line for each finger. Sketch the outline of the membrane.

Picture 3 Now you have the wing structure, highlight the bones by going over them with a thicker line.

Picture 4 Clean up the drawing and add detail to the membrane to bring out the skin's texture.

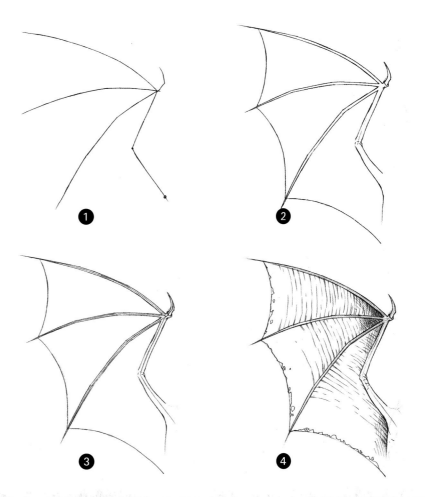

DRAGON

A dragon, from the Greek word 'drakon' meaning 'serpent', is an enormous, formidable beast. Dragons live in underground lairs filled with priceless, glittering treasures they have collected over centuries. Their huge wings and fiery breath make them terrifying adversaries.

1

Start with the stick figure. Draw an S-shaped body and lines for the wings. You also need a circle for the head and two cuboids for the jaws.

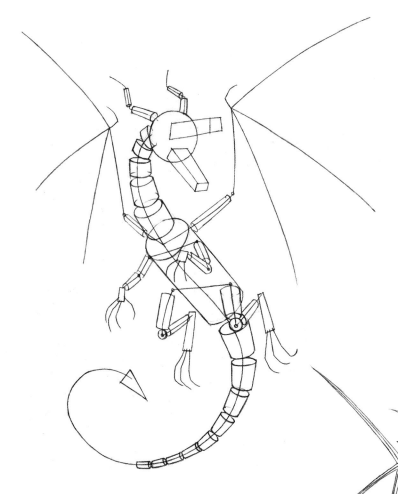

2

Add the rest of the construction shapes, using cylinders for the neck, body and tail. Draw wider shapes for the thicker end of the tail and neck, and narrower shapes for the end of the tail and where the neck joins the head.

3

Improve the head and add the skin by drawing around the shapes. At this stage you can also add the claws.

4
Develop the wings by drawing connection lines between the bone supports. Erase your construction shapes, then add detail to the underbelly. Make the teeth look uneven and irregular.

Check out page 7 for tips on how to draw a dragon's wings.

5

Clean up the drawing and add detail to the skin and the wings. Try to create a torn, papery effect at the wing edges. Don't forget to include the fire coming out of the dragon's mouth.

6
Now your pencil drawing is finished, you need to ink it over for a more dramatic effect.

7

Bring your dragon to life by adding colour. Start by applying a beige base to the whole drawing.

Build up layers using a sandy colour followed by grey on the belly and underside of the neck and wings.

For the upper body, use orange and dirty red. You can create dirty red by mixing red with a little grey.

BASILISK

The title of 'king of the serpents' belongs to the basilisk. It is the largest snake the world has ever known, although its ferocious head is bird-like rather than serpentine. Its breath is poisonous, but its deadliest weapons are its piercing eyes: a single glance is fatal to anything it looks at.

1
Start with an S-shape to create the snake-like body. Include a circle for the head.

2
Draw the construction shapes
using different-sized balls along
the length of the body. Plot out the
basilisk's beak with two triangles.

3
Create a smooth form over the
shapes by adding the skin.
Then draw the ferocious head.
In mythology, the basilisk has
the head of a cockerel with
sharp teeth, demonic eyes
and a wild crest.

❹

Remove the construction shapes and add lines for the belly. Draw the outer scales using the brick method to create a scaly, snake-like skin.

The brick method for creating scales is described on page 6.

TOP TIP
For light shading, draw fine slanted lines close together rather than shading in a solid block.

5
Complete the pencil drawing by adding detail to the head and body. Include light shading on the eyes, beak and crest.

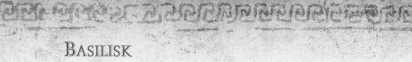

6

Now ink over the drawing. Keep the eye socket dark to make it look scary and add heavier patches to the crest to give it depth.

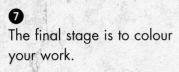

7

The final stage is to colour your work.

Use a light grey base for the beak followed by buttercup yellow and rusty orange.

Colour the underbelly with a beige base layer. Then add light grey.

Build up the colours on the crest with layers of orange and red. Use mid-grey to create darker areas.

The scales have a warm red base followed by a darker red and dark grey for shading.

MEDUSA

The Medusa's hair of writhing snakes marks her as a gorgon, a type of reptile-woman in Greek mythology. Any living creature she looks at turns instantly to stone. However Medusa has a weakness which is not shared by her two sisters. Of all the gorgons, she alone is mortal.

1
Begin with the stick figure.
Draw the looping body carefully.
Don't forget the hands.

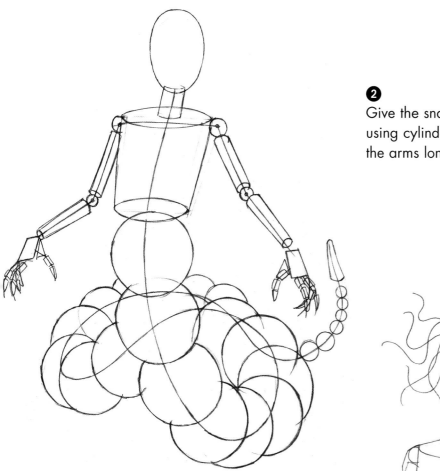

2

Give the snake-like body 3D form using cylinders and balls. Make the arms long and thin.

3

Now draw Medusa's hideous face. Her hair is a mass of writhing snakes, so add S-shapes to her head to create this effect. Give her body an outline and develop her clawed hands.

4

Remove the construction shapes, then draw the scales on the body. Add the necklace, bangles and headdress. Improve Medusa's hair by giving the snakes an outline and drawing their heads.

Find out how to draw snakes' heads close up on page 6.

5

Add detail to the face and heavy shading around the eyes. Use lighter shading on the body and arms. To create the scales on the snake-head hair, use the cross-hatching method.

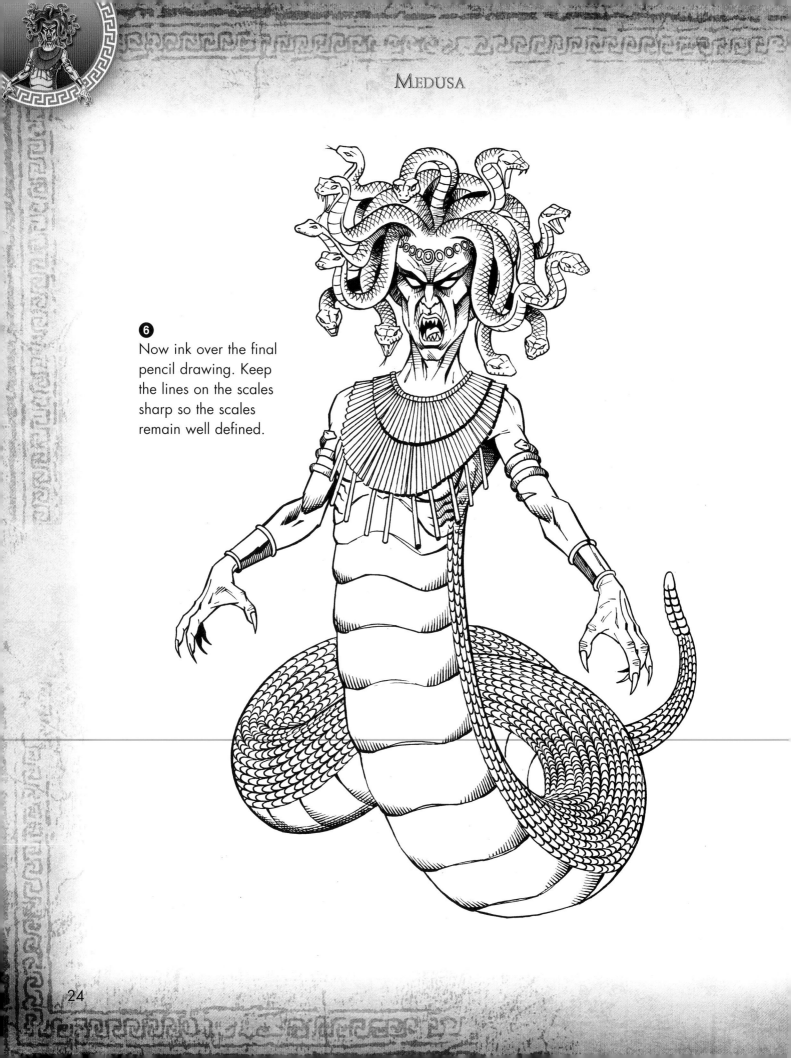

6 Now ink over the final pencil drawing. Keep the lines on the scales sharp so the scales remain well defined.

7 You can bring out Medusa's fierceness and snake-like qualities when you colour your art.

A pale skin tone has been used for the head and arms followed by layers of pale green and grey.

Colour the gold jewellery with a yellow base. Add yellow ochre and orange to create darker tones.

The main body has a pale olive base of yellow and grey.

The scales are grass green and emerald green followed by dark green. You can make green darker by adding dark grey.

25

CREATING A SCENE: THE DRAGON'S LAIR

Many myths and legends tell of adventurers doing battle with dragons in caves deep beneath the earth. As jealous, greedy creatures, dragons are attracted to underground hoards of precious metals. But woe betide anyone foolish enough to try to creep up on a sleeping dragon and snatch some treasure – because these giant reptiles often sleep with one eye open!

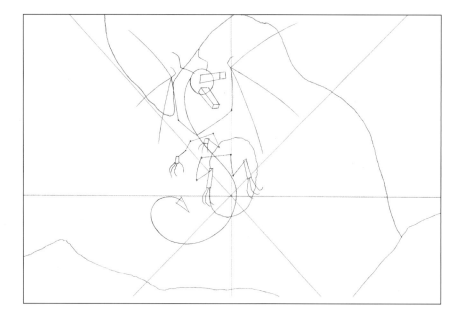

1 Perspective is not absolutely vital to this scene, as the action is set inside a cave. However you still need to add a vanishing point to give the effect that the dragon's lair extends deeper into the mountain. Note that the horizon is not exactly central. This adds height to the image.

2 With the basic shape of the lair defined by your first lines, start to add more definition to the rock formations and stalactites. Not only does this flesh out detail; it also helps to begin to build depth into your images.

3 Add more detail to the rock formations of the lair. Try to avoid uniformity in the layout of the lines to make a more natural looking rock.

4 Add shadowing and texture to the rocks and gold hoard. Always bear in mind the direction of your light source, as this is critical to making the image of the dragon and the background appear to be part of the same illustration.

5 Shadow and texture play a very important role in the inking stage of this lair. Keep your fill-ins light and build up gradually as it is always easier to add depth of texture than it is to take it away. Ensure your lining on the rocky areas is kept sharp to reinforce the impression of jagged and dangerous rocks.

6 This dank and dingy underground lair has very little light coming in, although the treasure still glints brightly in the gloom. Use green and blue shades in the background to make it feel cold and unwelcoming. The addition of mossy tones suggests that it is an abandoned location in which a dragon would feel at home.

GLOSSARY

cross-hatching
A shading technique where criss-crossing diagonal lines are overlapped to make an area of shadow.

cuboid
An object that has six faces like a cube.

cylinder
A shape with circular ends and straight sides.

membrane
A thin sheet or skin which is part of a living organism.

perspective
Changing the size and shape of objects in an artwork to create a sense of nearness or distance.

uniformity
The quality of being consistently the same and unchanging.

vanishing point
The point at which the lines showing perspective in a drawing meet each other.

woe
Great sadness.

INDEX

WEBSITES

http://www.elfwood.com/farp/art.html
A collection of articles about drawing characters and scenes from myth and fantasy.

http://drawsketch.about.com/od/drawfantasyandscifi/tp/imagination.htm
Advice on drawing from your imagination.